Soft Skills For Young Pros

A Synthesis of Opinions from 45 Thriving Millennials

Reet Sen

Foreword

Dear Friend,

Welcome to *Soft Skills For Young Pros.*

For those entering today's market, it doesn't take long to figure out that winning and losing in the real world is far different to passing or failing in school or university. There are fewer compliments, your grades don't land your dream job, and there's no such thing as a participation trophy.

The aim of this book is to bridge the gap between what we are taught in higher education and the skills we need to thrive in the real world. This book represents opinions from 45 thriving young pros, whom I've interviewed personally. In conducting these interviews, I've attempted to attain as diverse a spread of opinions as possible. Interviews were conducted both formally, and informally, individually and in groups. The challenge lied in digging into the most interesting opinions while ensuring an even demographic representation. Given the diversity of the respondents, conflicting opinions were inevitable. However, it was interesting to see how much the internet has broken down barriers between right and wrong, and good and bad. The issues mentioned in this book are the most relevant and consistent themes across the responding body.

If you are in university, higher education, or a young professional, this book is a must read.

Acknowledgements

Mum and Dad, your unwavering support is an absolute blessing. My sister Ronja, you've provided several stories for me to choose from and include within the chapters. Sorry if any haven't been approved! My partner Vanessa, your patience and support throughout the process has been absolutely incredible, and something I couldn't have done without. I appreciate you.

In addition, I'd like to thank the following thriving young pros, who graciously took part in interviews:

Dr Arka Roy - Professor of Statistics at Bowling Green State University

Julian Baladurage - CoFounder at MBJ London / UK Young Entrepreneur of the Year 2015

Damu Winston - Founder of ULIQ Language App

Chris Schelzi - Full-Stack Marketer

Caroline Beaton - Writer & Speaker: Psychology of Millennials at Work / Contributor at Forbes Magazine

Gabriela Goldenstein - Sr Brand Manager at Nike / Organising Committee at the Rio Olympics

Bryan Teare - Host of the Quarter Life Comeback Podcast

Preetam Sen - Director, Partnership Sales at Manchester City Football Club

Viviane Barretto - Management Consultant / Analyst at Accenture

Daniel Payares - Electrical Engineer / MBA

Ana Gutierrez - Project Manager in Telecom Industry

Chesterphil Tangga-an - Business Manager at Siemens Healthcare

Carlos Torres - Private Equity & Venture Capitalist

Sarika Mirchandani - Recent MBA Graduate

Brian Arpie - Software Engineer / Ranked Chess Player / Professional Poker Player

Andrew Smith - People & Culture Advisor

Tony Ibrahim - Operations Manager

Angus Goulding - Personal Trainer / Gym Owner

Karina Halfen - Change Management Specialist

Tarek ElSheikh - Finance VP

Cameron Stallard - Real Estate Director

Matthew Leeman-War - Economist / Pro Mixed Martial Artist

Anna Wood - Product Marketing Specialist

Naveen Verghese - Actor / Internet Celebrity

Carmen Bilbao - Digital Transformation Consultant

Hersh Thaker - Innovation Specialist at Shell UK

Shamir Bharmal - Operations Strategist

Natasha Raju - Digital Marketing Specialist

Tim Beckers - Credit Controller

Louisa Massey - Speech Pathologist

Charlie Murray - Corporate Presales Consultant

Michael Weatherley - Legal Associate

David Rodriguez Sanchez - CEO & Founder of FoodForAll

Nick Merican - Aviation Engineer / Implementation Manager

Rob Parker - Content Marketing Strategist

Travis William - Online Business Strategist

Jorge Diaz - Commercial Banking Specialist

Detina Zalli - Lecturer in Biomedical & Clinical Science / Harvard Post-Doc Graduate

Contents

Chapter One:

My Story

"The most valuable skill-set I've found in my transition is the ability to use 'soft skills'. More than the technical knowledge, which can be taught, Youtubed or Googled, soft skills will help you optimise the time you spend at work, build great relationships and enhance career fulfilment. It's a skill-set I've found to be virtually irreplaceable."

Having travelled to 28 different countries, lived in 6, and worked professionally in Australia, USA and the UK, I now feel like I've scratched a major itch, which confronted me three years ago.

I grew up, studied and worked in Brisbane, Australia - a large but lowly populated city. At aged 24, I found myself sinking into a professional and social comfort zone. I was working as a Business Development Executive at an e-learning/ tech company. I was learning a lot. I was being challenged. And I had responsibility. But I wasn't fractionally as motivated as I am about my career today.

I was living at home so wasn't worried about paying bills and was very much living in my comfort zone. Many of my friends were also in a similar situation – Two years out of an undergrad degree, working a decent job, living at home, and saving up for a house. They were content.

And why not? It seems like a good position to be in, right?

I wasn't content.

I had a lot going for me but still found myself staring down the barrel of a quarter life crisis. I felt stuck. Stuck in the comfort of my values, beliefs, and in the comfort of my social and professional eco-chamber. What I knew for sure was one thing - I wasn't going to accept this as my path in my career or in life.

I decided I needed change of environment. I felt a burning desire to travel, but I didn't want to spend my time in jobs that did not match my career ambitions. I'd always considered an MBA for professional reasons and now I had nothing to lose.

My intention was to immerse in an environment of professional and cultural diversity. Hult International Business School, was renowned for it's dedication to international experience and was FT voted to have the most international MBA program. It had campuses in Boston, New York, London, San Francisco, Dubai and Shanghai, and offered the unique opportunity for its students to rotate. This was ultimately a big part of my decision to join the program. Boston, Massachusetts became my home for the following year.

People have different reasons for doing an MBA or higher education of any kind. For some, it's seen as a natural step in accelerating their career. For others it's a gateway to becoming a well-rounded professional. And for some it's an excuse to spend a year or two partying. Either way, it's a big investment of time and money. For me, the objective was to find some direction in my career and accelerate my learning curve. People ask me all the time if it was a worthwhile investment. My answer is in two parts:

Financially, *I'm still finding out.*

Intangibly, *absolutely.*

I've gained 10x more self awareness and have a far better understanding of my strengths and weaknesses. I've been fortunate to also have built a great network throughout my travels and projects.

Most importantly, I've gained a sense of direction in my career. Here are three things I hold as my personal imperatives in career prospects:

1. **Dealing With People:** whether it's leading a team or influencing decisions.

2. **Travel:** In addition to a desire to work with different cultures, I'm not one who enjoys sitting at my desk day after day. I much prefer the desk one day, a different city or client's site the next, and then my home office the following day. I've learnt I love freedom and flexibility.

3. **To Tap-Dance To Work Every Day:** (As Warren Buffet puts it) In simple terms, I like to be able to work each day like it's my own business, even if I'm working for someone else.

Now living in London, I'm pursuing a genuine passion for marketing, sales and entrepreneurship at Edtech company, Full Fabric. I travel to various university campuses around Europe to demonstrate new ways in which university managers can optimise their student recruitment and marketing strategies. I love being able to offer solutions to widespread internal issues, and tap dance to work every day like I'm working on my own company.

The most valuable skill-set I've found in my transition is the ability to use 'soft skills'. More than the technical knowledge, which can be taught, Youtubed or Googled, soft skills will help you optimise the time you spend at work, build great relationships and enhance career fulfilment. It's a skill-set I've found to be virtually irreplaceable.

At work, in higher education and throughout my career, I've studied the transition of millennials at work. The next few chapters are dedicated to these lessons and observations.

Along my journey, I was fortunate to connect with some of the more insightful people in our generation, from the Young Entrepreneur of the Year in 2015 and Forbes writers, to PhD professors and Rio Olympic executives.

In writing this book, I interviewed over 40 high achieving millennials. That being said, my intention for this book is not only to reflect on my own knowledge and experience but that of people who have actually hit it big in today's workplace. Granted, how you define 'hitting it big' is subjective. You probably know many people who are making an immense amount of money but complain relentlessly about the stresses of their job and how their life is out of balance. These are *not* the insights I aim to bring to you, but rather the ideas of those who have found a sense of purpose.

In addition to my personal insights into the soft skills worth building in 2017, in upcoming chapters you will read thoughts and opinions of people who have found careers through entrepreneurship or employment. What they have in common is one thing - career fulfillment.

Chapter Two:

Defining Soft Skills

"Every day, we are challenged to deal with people of all ages, positions and cultural backgrounds. I strive to show the same level of respect for everyone, from the janitor to the CEO. It's the best way I know how to have the trust and confidence from those around me, and it keeps me happy at work"

Gabriela Goldenstein - Senior Brand Manager at Nike / RIO 2016 Organising Committee

If you've ever spoken with clients, co-workers, university peers, if you've ever led a project or a sporting team, chances are you have used soft skills. Soft skills, in simple terms, are the way in which we interact with our environment.

This is often used interchangeably with Emotional Quotient (EQ). While IQ refers to our technical skills and general intelligence, EQ is a cluster of our communication, personality traits, language, optimism, and friendliness, that describe our relationship with others. In addition to EQ traits, which predominantly refer to how we deal with people, soft skills also considers how we manage ourselves in response to other stimulus. They account for our productivity, stress management and intuitive decision making.

Some of the world's leading professions require its practitioners to exhibit an immense amount of soft skills. These skills apply just about everywhere. If you are a university professor, the content you teach are typically the hard facts of your subject. The ways you deliver this information are dictated by your soft skills. The way you communicate them and the way you make your students understand them; these are your soft skills. Whether you're a doctor, lawyer, business-person or team athlete, chances are you will need to apply your version of soft skills to be successful. Many of the world's leaders, like: Martin Luther King, Muhammad Ali, Nelson Mandela, Mahatma Gandhi, exhibited an incredible level of soft skills, which they used to initiate change, influence decisions and touch the lives of so many.

Of course, these skills can also be used for evil. We also hear about the travesty induced by Saddam Hussein, Bin Laden and Hitler.

Muhammad Ali was a great boxer. But he wasn't necessarily a technician. Unlike Joe Frazier, Floyd Patterson and many of his other opponents, he wasn't ever known for his technical soundness. It was a surprise to many in his time as to how he used his unconventional style to destroy opponent after opponent. Upon studying his many books and documentaries, I was fascinated by the tremendous level of soft skills that Ali exhibited both inside and outside the ring. He used his exuberant personality and self-confidence to get inside his opponents' minds and reel them into his own style of boxing. He would trash-talk and publicly gloat about how badly he would defeat each of his opponents. He would do this before each fight to psych out each of his opponents. Fortunately, he was a skilled enough boxer to back up his words during each fight. But more often than not, the fight was won before it even started.

In parallel, Ali leveraged his in-ring success and exuberant personality to fight for human rights. He articulated his beliefs with charisma and conviction to his fans and media personnel. This won him an incredible amount of supporters, and a hell of a lot of back-lash. Most importantly, to this day Ali starts conversations about what's right and wrong in humanity. If it wasn't for Ali's soft skills, he wouldn't be nearly as influential as an athlete or public figure.

For young pros, our soft skills dictate our ability to find a job, lead a team or start a business. These factors ultimately dictate how much money we make, the quality of our relationships, and our overall fulfillment.

The following chapters will reflect the knowledge and experience of over 40 successful millennials who I've had the chance to interview, either formally or informally. The chapters are intended to bridge the gap between what we're taught in college and university, and essential skills we need to thrive in the workplace.

Moving forward, you will learn the following:

- The number one challenge you'll face as a young pro (if you haven't already)
- The biggest mistake you can make your early career, and how to avoid it
- How to differentiate between constructive and destructive criticism in your 20's
- Why you should invest a large chunk of your time in building your network

- Networking strategies in 2017
- How to be a good leader in your 20's

Chapter Three:

The Number One Challenge

"The biggest challenge was realizing that my passions don't equal my purpose. I thought that once I found a way to do all my passions full-time, I would be happily ever after. But I actually felt unfulfilled. This led me to working on a book on millennial purpose: why aren't we getting the one thing we set out for? The book, in addition to getting crystal clear on my mission and resilience, has made me more fulfilled."

Caroline Beaton - Millennial Psychology Journalist / Writer at Forbes, Huffington Post

Of the 45 respondents that I've interviewed, the biggest challenges faced by the majority of them in their career stem from one thing - a disconnect between one's passion and purpose. This disconnect is the root cause of your quarter life crisis, degree change and the reason you job hop.

What is the difference between passion and purpose?

One of my respondents is Forbes' writer and millennial expert Caroline Beaton. Caroline put it best in her Forbes article, captioned *What No One Told Me About Following My Passion.* She says, "Passion, the way many millennials define it, is self-oriented. Passion is a strong inclination toward a self-defining activity that one loves, values and in which one invests a substantial amount of time and energy."

Caroline went on to explain that purpose is 'other-oriented' and largely intertwined with an individual's desire to seek connection with others.

What we can gauge by this explanation is that your passion seeks short term pleasures for yourself. Your purpose however, craves a larger connection with those around you, giving back through connection or some sort of service, whether it's entertainment, charitable service, business solution or saving lives.

Lionel Messi grew up wanting to be a football player all his life. Despite challenges and adversities, he made it to Barcelona FC and is now arguably the best striker in the world.

I would imagine Messi to have been very passionate about soccer as a child. In his teens and into the early part of his career, a lot of cards were dealt his way. With a lot of favours, a heap of luck, and an incredible amount of hard work and dedication, he managed to make it happen.

The unfortunate things is, if you consider the other kids growing up with burning passion to become professional football players, the percentage who actually end up playing for teams like Barcelona, Manchester United, Real Madrid, the percentage is quite low.

What happens to those who don't make it? Those who cannot fulfill their passions?

What do you do when there's a disconnect between your passion and your purpose?

I interviewed UK Young Entrepreneur of the year, Julian Baladurage in an attempt to shed some light on this.

Critical Self-Assessment

Julian is 28 years of age. Over the last 5 years, he has built a WaaS business with 3 offices around the world, employing 37 people.

I asked him what he felt was the key to his entrepreneurial success. His response was: critical self-assessment. To be able to understand your own strengths and weaknesses - double down on your strengths and accept your weaknesses.

Imagine you want to start your own business. If you're great with people, you might be better as an entrepreneur, salesman or marketer, than an accountant, developer or web-designer. Do you then decide to build a base level understanding of this other stuff?

The truth is, you could. But you probably wouldn't be too motivated by it. Outsourcing these, or partnering with people who are capable of holding up these pillars will ensure you keep your sanity, and have more time to master your sales and marketing. Messi didn't become one of the best strikers by trying to be a 'well-rounded athlete'. He went all in on one skill - finding the back of the net.

"With a firm understanding of your own skill-set and consciously being adaptive you'll be able to differentiate between good and bad advice."

Stay Humble, Stay Grounded

A large part of my discussion was about the importance of managing your psychology. The business world - and the world in general - can be volatile. You can go from top of the world into a dark valley in a matter of months, weeks, days.

How do you stomach your losses and keep yourself sane?

According to Julian, no situation is as bad as it seems in your mind. Humans have a negative bias, which takes over when they make a mistake. The solution is going back to basics, think long and hard about the mistake you've made and why it's causing anxiety. Ink what you think. Write down the actual consequences versus how you perceive it. Do this well and you'll find the lesson. Take the lesson and run with it - don't think about the mistake again.

The other side of the coin is that feeling of euphoria, which makes you feel absolutely invincible. You might've been promoted, closed a large deal or been drafted to a big league. You go out and buy yourself a couple of new suits, a Rolex watch, and drinks at the bar for strangers.

If this is you, be careful. These "high" moments can lead to a series of bad decisions. According to Julian, enjoy the highs, but be conscious you're not getting carried away. It's a slippery slope.

Get Really Good at Your Strengths, Start *NOW*

After you've self-assessed yourself, outsource the other stuff and get to work. If you work/study from 9 to 6, ask yourself how you spend your 6 to 12. To master your craft, you'll need to dedicate time after hours.

I've been trying to get really good at written and spoken communication. For months leading up to writing this book, I had been writing blogs for my website and Linkedin. I had been interviewing and networking with thriving millennials to get content for my blog (www.reetsen.com). After six months of hustle, I finally got the infrastructure I needed to write this book. Which by the way, I wrote after 6pm on work days and on weekends.

Sure, I've definitely been guilty of watching trash TV, excessive partying and procrastinating. This has caused me to compromise not only working on my skill-set but also things I value such as working out, spending time with family, and exploring my hobbies.

There are also things I wish I prioritised over others when I was 18 - simple things like listening to a podcast instead of the same old rap playlist. Had I prioritised in everything like I do today, I know I would've seen a net gain at aged 26.

The advantage of being a millennial?

It's not too late to start.

Time is on our side. What we do at 18, shapes how we think at 26. What we do at 26, shapes how we think at 34. Get really good at something. Start now by prioritising your biggest asset - time.

I have done my own self awareness assessment. I know that I am enthusiastic about sales and marketing. I'm a promoter, I'm a campaigner, and I'm also a writer.

I want to do good for young professionals. That's who I want to serve. This is why I work in higher education and this is why I write this book. However, unlike many other people in my profession, I'm more of an introvert. Although the introvert in me loves going into deep thought and ideation, the promoter in me needs to share these. As a result, blogging, writing and speaking becomes a necessity and a source of satisfaction.

So let's apply this to the Messi example.

I can imagine Messi figuring out he has something unique to offer to the game of soccer. I imagine he would have lived and breathed soccer from a young age. He's probably made mistakes and suffered injuries and setbacks, but has stayed humble and grounded. Today, he's arguably the best football player in the world.

What about the kids who played with Lionel in the park, or the ones who trained in his club team?

They too are just as passionate about football and dream to play for FC Barcelona or Real Madrid. They too want to chase their passion. But reality is, not everyone gets the call-up.

What to do next?

Refer to your strengths. Find your purpose.

A good friend of mine, Preetam Sen grew up in Boston playing basketball at school level. It was his passion. However, he recognised his purpose to be slightly different. It was dictated by his strengths - he's a great salesperson, entrepreneurial and a peoples' person. He capitalised on this, but was committed to staying aligned with the sports industry.

The result?

After a bit of patience and huge dedication, he was appointed Head of Sponsorship at Brooklyn Nets. Today, he's crushing it as the Director of American Sponsorships at Manchester City Football Club.

Chapter Four:

The Biggest Mistake You Can Make

"The biggest mistake I've made is to pursue what others view as success, and not what I view as success."

Matthew Lee-Manwar - Pro MMA Athlete / Economist

"The biggest mistake I've made is being too passive. I understood for me, there was a cultural element to it but I learnt very quickly it's not the way forward in today's day and age."

Dr. Arka Roy - MBA Professor

One question I asked all of my respondents is,
"What is the biggest mistake you've made in your career?"

I'm personally of the opinion that this was one of the most important questions, simply because knowing what today's thriving millennials view as a key mistake will enable you to avoid it.

About one-third of my respondents answered along the lines of being too passive. Passiveness has caused people to do things which they never really wanted to do. This includes choosing the wrong business partner, buying into what friends and family view as success, not trusting their gut, accepting the wrong job, and grabbing the first offer that comes their way.

How can we avoid being passive? I believe it comes with the understanding that it is ok to say no. The realisation that it is your own life and you're entitled to protect your values.

Your friends, family and mentors mean well for you but at the end of the day, you have to trust your gut and double down on your strengths - no one knows your strengths like you do.

In her interview as a guest at Stanford University, Oprah Winfrey was asked about how she figured out she wanted to be a talk show host. Her response - sometimes knowing what you don't want to do is the best guide to uncovering what you do want to do.

In her 20's, Oprah was a news reporter and television anchor. As she explains it, this was seen as a "glamorous job" in those times. However, she felt it wasn't her "true thing".

She explains that the first time she was exposed to a talk show environment as a guest, it immediately felt like home. She decided immediately that she was going to pursue a career in talk show.

She went on to explain how she was valued, but mistreated at her news reporting job. She was underpaid and was shut down each time she approached her boss to discuss a pay rise. However, she knew it was a stepping stone to get to her true goal.

She managed to turn the tables on her employer when she handed in her resignation. At first, her colleagues and boss tried to convince her she would fail in the talk-show world. Then, she was being offered double her salary, a car and an apartment, all fully paid for!

She declined all of it. *She was assertive.*

In the 90's, the talk show culture was to create confrontational television. It was a common intention to expose celebrities of their controversies, interview extremists groups, expose adulterers, and overall create humiliation to increase TV ratings.

Oprah had bought into the hype for a period of time. However, after seeing her guests get humiliated time after time, she ultimately decided 'no more'. Instead of letting television use her, she was going to use television to create positive vibes for her viewers guests, and herself. She was assertive.

Today, we know Oprah Winfrey as an activist, philanthropist and the greatest talk show host of all time.

Often, the best way to discover your strengths or a career of purpose, is to first understand what's not for you. By being assertive and saying no to the things that are not aligned with your values, you open yourself up to opportunities that are more fulfilling.

Chapter Five:

Differentiating Between Constructive & Destructive Criticism

"The skill lies in understanding what input to turnaround and which to ignore. How to pick the good from the bad advice, without compromising your company culture or personal values."

Julian Baladurage - Co-Founder & CEO of MBJ Technologies / UK Young Entrepreneur of the Year 2015

"Constructive criticism aims to help others grow and become better professionals while destructive criticism aims to highlight the bad things to prove that you are better. Being able to identify what is in your control, what is not and being able to communicate this is how I typically handle both."

David Rodriguez Sanchez - CEO & Founder of FoodForAll (Food Recycling App)

As kids, we are taught to be good sportsmen / sportswomen and accept criticism gracefully. Like many of our childhood lessons, this is one that has become lost in translation as we've progressed into our 20's.

Having been fortunate enough have travelled to 28 different countries and lived in 6. As a result, I've observed the social and cultural elements that play a part in the way criticism is interpreted. I've seen alpha egos snap like pit-bulls at the slightest hint of criticism and the overly passive personas who will compromise everything to please people - often at the cost of rejecting their own values.

In a social world and global economy, it is increasingly difficult to strike the right balance between having the humility to accept constructive criticism, and having the confidence to show a figurative middle finger.

These are some lessons I have picked up through travel, education, and meeting like-minded people and those who aren't.

1. Remember They're Human - Just Like You

Do not underestimate anyone, or put anyone on a pedestal.

Whether it is our partner, clients, boss or best friend, if we give a person too much social or hierarchical power, we are essentially giving them control over our confidence. In my opinion, any criticism that puts a lasting dent in our confidence is destructive. Be open to criticism, but take it with a grain of salt.

Whether you're in an organisation, sporting team or the cadet force, when you're in a position of assumed leadership it is much harder to accept criticism or feedback from subordinates. Imagine you are the Chief of the army and your troops give you feedback from the battlefield. Would you accept it or dismiss it because it's coming from the bottom?

Often times, the information you need to avoid disaster comes from the ground-up.

2. The Comfort-Zone Test

My personal strategy to differentiate between constructive and destructive criticism is to see how far the critic ventures outside of their comfort zone.

As a by-product immersing in various cultures, I have had many of my beliefs challenged to the core. I have learnt that our beliefs are only a thesis until they are tested.

Consequently, I have learnt to dismiss criticism from people who live in their comfort zone or have skewed perceptions of the world.

Want to get out of your comfort zone?

Try this. Pick one of your beliefs. Challenge it.

Get a piece of paper. And write down all the reasons you could be flawed in this belief. See if you still feel the same way. For example, if you think credit cards are a bad source of debt, find out all the ways that you can leverage credit card debt to manage a better quality of life.

This is an exercise which would hugely challenge your beliefs. If you don't mind doing this, I welcome you to give me feedback or point out holes in my game.

3. The Walk-A-Mile Factor

Can your critic walk a mile in your shoes? Whatever your journey is, there will be people who have been there and done that. In this case it is valuable to actively ask for feedback and seek out constructive criticism. As mentioned in the previous chapter, we're better off learning from other people's mistakes than by making them ourselves. It saves us time and money. For this reason, I ensure I see a bit of myself in all the mentors that I seek out.

Your mentors must be relatable to you. Don't take business advice from your friend who hasn't paid a bill before. Don't take relationship advice from your friend who hasn't been in one. Be careful who you look up to.

Chapter Six:

The Biggest Investment You Can Make

> "It's not what you know, it's not who you know, it's who endorses you."
>
> **Damu Winston - CEO & Founder of ULIQ Language App**

The biggest investment you can make as a young pro is in people. By investing in people, you're opening yourself up to mentorship, future business opportunities and moral support.

The number one thing to keep in mind during this process, is people don't recall how smart or how impressive you are. People only recall how you make them feel. Actions are more impressive than words in every society. The most impressive thing you can do in every interaction is to make the other person feel good!

Here are three simple ways you can invest in other people:

Ask Good Questions

The most off-putting thing for me when I speak to a younger person, is when they're adamant about proving how smart they are. I'm more impressed by the quality of the questions that you ask, than what you read about the stock market or the property prices or the presidential election.

The quality of your question says a lot of about you and your character. It shows how understanding and interested you are, and how much empathy you can exhibit. Ultimately, it's a reflection of both your general and emotional intelligence. Instead of trying to prove how smart you are, just ask good questions!

Pay Attention

I'm even more impressed by how you make me feel during the interaction - the fact that you remember my name, my hobby or something I may have explained in an online article. If I'm going to be in your network or circle of influence, I have to first have positive vibes about you as a person. The way you can have this impression is simple - just make me feel good!

It's the little things that matter. Remember things that people have told you and reference them in later meetings and communications. It exhibits an attention to detail. You'll be amazed how much people will appreciate you if you remember things about them.

Have you ever had this happen to you?

You're walking down the street and cross paths with someone you've met before. You're smiling at them. They know you're smiling at them. They respond by avoiding eye contact or even looking in your general direction.

Congratulations! you've just deleted me from your memory.

I know I've had this happen more than a handful of times..

Please, don't be that person.

Make Introductions

One of the benefits of investing in other people is that you can introduce them to one another and add value to each of their lives.

Don't be afraid to introduce people in your circle of influence others who may benefit from meeting him or her. It shows that you're genuinely interested in helping the other person, and indirectly showcases the quality of your network. The easiest way to offer value is indirectly.

Note: Don't make an introduction and expect something in return. Be genuinely interested and genuinely helpful.

Chapter Seven

The Number One Skill for The Young Pro

"Identify what gets you excited. If it's an absolute burning desire, Block out the noise from others and go for it."

Preetam Sen - Director of Partnerships at Manchester City Football Club

> "The ability to make meaningful connections with others and finding a way to add value to those people before needing anything in return, is the most important skill."
>
> *Bryan Teare - Host of the Quarter-Life Comeback Podcast*

I posed two common questions to all of my respondents.

The first was, what do you believe to be the most important soft skill for Millennials in today's workplace?

The second was, if you were to write a letter to your 18-year-old self and include three pieces of advice, what would they be?

The responses I got were by and large along the lines of figuring out what excites you, making connections in this area and working for free to access mentors in the area.

At first, I wasn't able to classify this line of response. Upon throwing the question back at a few of the respondents, we classed this as "skilled networking". Not simply networking, but "skilled networking".

To do this right, you will need to first follow the steps outlined in Chapter 3.

Let me explain with an example.

My sister recently reached out to me asking for some advice. She is 21 years of age, on the verge of finishing university, and graduating law school. All her peers are currently in the process of trying to line up their careers. So her question was about a friend who recently graduated with a business degree.

Her friend is trying to find herself a job. I asked her, "What is she doing?"
My sister responded saying, "Well she's networking."
I said, "What exactly is she doing in terms of networking?"
Her response was, "You know, She's just connecting around on Linkedin..."

I thought to myself, what a low percentage way to go about a job hunt. Here's someone who is randomly sending connection requests on Linkedin and messaging them in hopes to get invited for an interview. She doesn't know which industry she wants to work in, or which function she wants to be involved in. She just wants to land herself a job in a company because it seems like the natural next step after graduating from university. This approach is no different to blasting out your CV to all listings you come across on a career site.

Where there's no vision, there's no direction. Like shooting darts in the dark, if you hit the bull's eye, you probably got extremely lucky. Leaving things to luck is never the safest bet when it comes to your career.

The advice I shared is this.

1. At the very least, she needs to figure out the industries that she wants to get involved in, and create a short-list of these.

2. Within this list, she must figure out a couple of specific companies that she innately desires to work for. For example, if you want to work in the media industry, you might see yourself as a cultural fit in ESPN.

3. Next, create a short short-list of functions that match your skill-set. Make sure they are not too broad and as inter-related as possible. For example, sales, marketing, and account management.

By performing the above steps, you might find your dream job is something specific. Like, Digital Account Management at ESPN. Now, you're ready to engage in skilled networking, as opposed to connecting around.

To share an example of skilled networking, I can offer one of my own experiences.

I consider myself an avid reader and audio podcast listener. Leading up to my move to Boston for my MBA, one of the podcasts I used to follow was the James Swanwick show. James would interview experts on the topics of health, wealth, love and happiness in his podcast episodes, which spoke to me at that point in my life. He would interview industry leaders in each area and deliver this as content.

I was a big fan of the guy. He is originally from my hometown of Brisbane, Australia and he lives in Los Angeles, California. He's come from the same cloth as me and has built a life for himself in the US. As a 23 year old getting ready to take the leap to the US, his story resonated with me.

There was an occasion on which he tweeted that he was coming back to Brisbane to visit his family. I messaged him saying,
"Hi James, I've been keeping up with your podcast for the past 4 months. Really love your content. I'd love the chance to catch up with you when you're in town.. What can we do to catch up?"

To my surprise, he tweeted back, "Hi Reet, I'm hosting a meet-up at the Story Bridge Hotel. Come say hello!"

I arrived at the venue to find him all set up with his voice recorder in hand, recording a podcast episode with the other members of the meet-up group. Despite being a bit star-struck, I was put on the spot straight away as he held the recorder to my face, "hey mate! Introduce yourself to the listeners.."

Next thing I know, I'm talking about everything from an Australian's opinion of the NFL to my biggest fears, and declaring my thoughts to tens of thousands of listeners (thanks a lot James).

Overall, that was a thoroughly enjoyable experience - networking my way into the James Swanwick Show.

Of course we had more time to talk off-air. We had a chat about the big issue in my life at that point in time - my move to America. He offered me some comparisons and contrasts of his experience in living in Australia vs America, which I found very helpful. He offered me some very valuable introductions to people in Boston. He shared some of his social media strategies with the group, and I offered him some of my own tips. I told him if there's anything I can do to add value virtually, I'd be glad to help. He remembered that.

I emailed him, literally on my first day in the US.

I said, "James, I mentioned to you when we met that I'll be moving to the States. Well I'm here now. I want to get some American work experience under my belt. And I want to start today. Is there anything I can do for you virtually, that would add value to your business?"

He replied, "Hi Reet, I've been searching for a couple of interns to help me with some product launches / manage my social media. Would you be interested?"

I thought to myself, Heck yes, I'd be interested! The reason I was excited is, although I'd be working for free, I know I had found myself a mentor. I replied saying, "Sure, I'll be glad to help you with this. In return, will you teach me about the media business and personally mentor me?" He agreed. The following week, I started managing his social media, and he would contact me every so often to revisit / revise strategies.

That year, I was a digital "right hand man". James mentored me in business, including teaching me how to launch my own podcast for Hult. Even more valuable, in my opinion, are the introductions he made to me. These included some thriving young pros who have helped me in writing this book by taking part in interviews. I'm very grateful for that experience, and I credit it to nothing but some skilled networking - knowing who I align with, reaching out, and adding massive value.

In the coming chapters, we'll dive deeper into the topic of skilled networking, and look specifically at the 80/20 rule in networking, and explore some networking strategies in 2017.

Chapter Eight:

The 80/20 Rule in Networking

"It doesn't quite suit me to 'never eat alone' but I find that if you connect with the right people, there's a trickle down effect. It's quality over quantity."

Chris Schelzi - Full-Stack Marketing Consultant

Chris Schelzi works with authors and entrepreneurs and is well known for his work as a Full-Stack Marketer, personal branding expert, and various keynote and podcast appearances.

Over our one-on-one interview, Chris shared productivity hacks, book recommendations and the biggest golden nugget - his personal guide to investing in like-minded people. Off the cuff, he referred to it as the 80/20 rule in networking.

The 80/20 rule is formally known as the Pareto Principle. From a broad sense, it states that roughly 80% of all effect comes from 20% of all causes.

In business, 80% of revenue comes from 20% of clients.

In economics, 80% of the world's income is controlled by 20% of the world's wealthiest people.

In the Olympics, 80% of the medals are won by 20% of the participating countries.

The 80/20 rule can be applied to networking in the same way, with the provision that you have an end goal in mind.

Your own VIP Club

I first started building my personal brand while I was studying my MBA. I knew this meant more opportunities upon graduation, and a chance for me to apply some practical entrepreneurship principles.

Being James Swanwick's right-hand man, I was fortunate to be able to observe what he was doing for his own brand and replicate it on a smaller scale. I joined the *Hult Think Tank club* which was the school media club, dedicated to delivering captivating content to higher education students. I contributed guest posts to their magazines and launched the club's first podcast channel. I would attend various conferences and meet-ups, interview cool and interesting people, and deliver this content through these mediums. It was a lot of fun.

Throughout this time, I noticed something fascinating which stands true even today. Roughly 20% of my network were actively supporting me in this pursuit - introducing me to other interviewees, offering mentorship or sharing my content on social media. If I had a club, these would be my VIP.

In Chapter 6, we discussed how my interviews have suggested that the biggest investment to be made as a young pro is in other people. With this in mind, we must start with our own VIP club. If you owned a nightclub, who would you put on the guest list? Keep your eyes and ears open. Recognize the people who are paying attention. Find a way to thank them.

The Trickle-Down Effect

As a millennial with introverted tendencies, Chris's story resonated. I love the book, Never Eat Alone by Keith Ferrazzi. His strategies are sophisticated and highly practical, but I know my personality is vastly different to the NY Times Best Selling Author. To eat lunch with a different person each day or be out and about each night at conferences or dinners or to constantly be on my phone texting, tweeting, and emailing, all sounds very draining to me. So I apply the principles that match my style and "never eat alone" on a different scale.

Chris mentioned he is also more of an introvert. It was interesting for me to see how an introvert could be so well-networked. I asked him to share some strategies in connecting with new people - this is when he mentioned the trickle down effect of the 80/20 rule.

Imagine you're in a job hunt, either as a fresh graduate or just looking for a career change. When interviewing with various companies, in most cases they will have more than one interview round. Depending on the nature and size of the company, The first round is typically with a HR Manager and the second round is with a Director, CEO or someone with similar decision making status.

Knowing this, would you aim to first connect with the HR Manager or the Director?

For me, it's best to go straight to the top. By connecting with the director, chances are you'll get an immediate referral to the HR Manager. Because the recommendation is coming from the top, the HR Manager will most probably have a more favourable attitude towards your profile than other candidates. Your CV will be at the top of the pile, and you'll jump the queue for the next round of interviews. Of course, the next round will be a conversation with the Director who already knows about you, you've had interaction with him, and your profile has now been validated by the HR Manager. It's a simple, yet effective play. If you had followed the standard procedure, chances are you'd have to wait in line like everybody else. By making yourself known to the boss, you would've multiplied your chances of landing the job.

It's no secret that people at the top are connected with other people at the top. They have more influence and more mobility. If you can add value, you'll be well received.

— — —

Remember, it's not who you know, it's who endorses you.

With this mind, you don't need to exhaust yourself by connecting with as many people as you physically can. Just focus 80% of your networking energy on connecting with those that will endorse you, and benefit from the trickle down effect.

Chapter Nine:

Rise Of The Introverts

"Spend your time and money on things that will make your life better, rather than things that make you feel good. Develop relationships with people that will make you a better person and professional."

David Rodriguez Sanchez - CEO & Founder of FoodForAll (Food Recycling App)

If you're an introvert like me, chances are the idea of "networking" seems daunting. You probably experience anxiety before and after the event and the entire experience seems a bit draining. As introverts, we are deep thinkers. We don't mind spending time by ourselves and are able to produce some of our best work in isolation. At the same time, isolation can be our enemy. At times we crave connection, and giving and receiving.

It is my belief though that there has probably never been a better time for introverts excel in their careers. In a world where social networking is made easy by online mediums such as LinkedIn and Facebook, introverts now have a huge advantage over extroverts. Consider some of the world's leading entrepreneurs - Bill Gates, Elon Musk, and Mark Zuckerberg (ironically, the founder of the world's largest social networking site). It's fair to say none of the above are known to be the 'life of the party'.

As mentioned in a previous chapter, the introvert in me loves going into deep thought and ideation but the campaigner in me needs to share these. As a result, networking becomes a necessity and a source of satisfaction. Hence I'd like to share the following steps, which have worked for me in communicating my ideas and networking purposefully.

1. Think Strategic

When it comes to making contacts or connecting with mentors, it's rarely a case of "just because". Warren Buffet would make a great business mentor. But if your goal is to take part in the next Olympic track games, chances are he won't be of great help to you. Think of who you align yourself with. Once you've figured this out, consider accessibility.

You'd be farfetched trying to connect with Usain Bolt in a moment's notice. However, the sprints coach of your old high school team may be connected with the chairman of the National Sprints Academy, who may have hosted Usain Bolt to train at his facilities. With this in mind, it would make sense to reconnect with your high school sprints coach as a starting point.

As an example, I am actively trying to get my blog posts published on high traffic media sites such as Forbes, Inc., and Business Insider. Should I send my pieces directly to the editor?

For me, the answer to that is no. He or she has no idea who I am. With this in mind, I'm networking with fellow guest contributors on these sites. Perhaps they can teach me how they went about getting their work published. Or if I'm lucky, introduce me directly to the editor.

2. Harness Social Media

In today's digital age, networking conferences are not the be all end all. For better or worse, the playing field for social interactions has now moved online. This is great news for introverts. I love using Linkedin and Facebook to connect, and Instagram and Snapchat to share.

In terms of connection, it's quality over quantity. If you are connecting with someone on LinkedIn, be sure to personalise your request. If you are sending a cold email, be sure to offer something first before asking for anything in return. From experience, my personal reaction to a company or individual sending me a cold email is to delete it. Offer me a free service, content or trial, and then we'll talk.

Therefore, when connecting with guest posters, I would only reach out to authors whose articles resonate with me. It goes without saying that I'd have to read and understand the full article, and be in an intelligent position to provide valuable feedback.

3. Add Value

Once I've done my research to find out enough about the author and their article, I would then look for ways to add value. I find that my email response rates are a good KPI of how well I've performed the above steps and how much value I've added. From experience, detailed feedback on the sections that resonate with me the most, and other areas which fellow readers might also be interested in, generally gets me a much higher response rate than, 'I also write great content and was wondering if you'd be kind enough to introduce me to the editor of Forbes magazine.'

A week later, I would do the same critique of another article. I know authors love this feedback as it is enabling them to engage deeper with their audience and providing new topics for discussions. After the second or third critique, I have usually built up enough rapport to ask for an introduction to the editor. I am no longer a stranger. I have demonstrated credibility, added value, and can now comfortably ask for a favour.

Best-selling author, Keith Ferrazzi explains the importance of entering each interaction with the attitude of 'how can I help this person?' as opposed to 'how can this person help me?' But when you do receive a favour, a simple gesture like writing a Linkedin recommendation is a great way to express your gratitude.

— — —

It's my belief that the internet opens a huge window for introverted millennials in 2017. Many say we should push ourselves to get out there and immerse into social settings. I agree to an extent. But I also believe in self awareness and playing to our strengths. Since the opportunity is there to build business and connections digitally, why not capitalise?

Chapter Ten:

How To Be A Good Leader In Your 20's

"You'll always have to serve someone or something, regardless of whether you're in a job or self-employed. Decide who you want to serve. Commit to it."

Caroline Beaton - Millennial Psychology Journalist / Writer at Forbes, Huffington Post

> "Collaboration: I ask, ask, and ask again. This is the essence of sucking out the information from all your team members and putting them on the table. Try and you will be amazed of how much they know that you didn't."
>
> *Chesterphil Tangga'an - Business Division Manager at Siemens Healthcare*

Be a good follower.

Like many professionals in their 20's, I aspire to soon be in a position to lead people, and align them with my vision. I aspire to have my own office, a comfy chair, a nice view, and loyal team-mates in a dynamic work culture. I aspire to offer massive value, which my troops will rally around.

As such, I have paid special attention over the last seven or so years to the intricate details that make up a leader figure in an organisation or team setting, more specifically, the twenty-something year olds. I've observed graduate school teams, sporting teams, social groups, discussion groups and of course, the workplace. I've noticed a very specific set of traits which enables the twenty-something year old individual to become the leader in an environment where everyone else also aspires to be the leader.

Upon graduating my MBA, I was fortunate enough to be a part of the winning team of the Hult Global Consulting Challenge. The solution put forward by our team was to be implemented by Philips as part of their sustainability model, to better utilise lighting resources. Our team worked together for a full year and went through the typical forming, storming, and norming stages. Being the youngest (and least experienced) member of the team, I made a conscious effort to observe the dynamics while working with five of the more intellectual individuals in the program, four of whom were on the MBA Dean's List.

I was surprised to see that the person who took the leadership role in the program was not someone who we consciously elected into the leadership position. Nor was he someone that the rest of us placed on a pedestal for his intellect, charisma or popularity. On the contrary, this was a guy that did the simple things right, and rendered the best quality and fullest quantity in every team activity that he took part in.

His name was Alvaro Santos. In any team discussion, Alvaro would literally go around the table and ask for ideas from everyone else, while hardly ever contributing any of his own. His contributions during team meetings consisted of "Reet, what do you like about Carlos's idea?" or "what would you do to improve Tarik's solution?" In essence, his approach was to build on the team's ideas, as opposed to having his own heard.

Alvaro was a great follower. He would follow every single idea and try to find the value in them. As a result, it got to a point where the whole team would turn to him for the validation of each and every idea. Alvaro was indirectly voted team leader.

From experience in work groups, university teams, sports teams, and not-for-profit projects, these are some habits that I have seen illustrated from Alvaro and other young leaders I have been fortunate to work with:

Be on time and come prepared

Discipline is tough, but by maintaining it you give yourself credibility. Be the person who doesn't get thrown off by delays and distractions.

Set an agenda

Work with team-mates to agree on an agenda for every meeting. Be assertive about the agenda. Your team-mates will notice the increased productivity.

Take responsibility

Own up to your mistakes, statements and false assumptions. Commit yourself to team tasks.

Avoid pettiness

It's easy to get sucked into team politics. Stay above this. Help other team-mates do the same.

Include all, exclude none

In team discussions, ensure everyone is getting a chance to participate. There will invariably be larger personalities than others. Demonstrate equality by prompting the softer spoken individuals to share their thoughts.

Build on team ideas before proposing your own

Become a strong leader, by first being a good follower.

Chapter 11

Three Pieces of Advice For My 18-Year-Old Self

"There's no better time to follow our passions, as long as we don't neglect our purpose. So be resilient in creating your dream story, but be sure to balance it out with practicality."

If you were to leave a note for your 18 year old self, with three bits of advice, what would they be?

I had this question turned around on me for the first time while conducting a group interview with some young travelers in Nice, France. At the time, I was stumped. Despite evaluating dozens of responses from various people, I never stopped to answer this for myself. After a week of reflection, I went ahead and wrote a blog about this.

Here are the three pieces of advice I'd like to leave behind for the 8 years younger version of myself.

1. Network like a Rockstar

It's a shame that networking wasn't a "thing" when I started off at university. The idea was that you'd work hard at university and get good grades. At the end of your course you would apply to a grad scheme at a large multi-national corporation. The better your grades, the higher the chance of you getting an offer.

This idea didn't work for me for two reasons.

First, I wasn't an academic genius. I've always been a creative more than an academic. And I certainly wasn't motivated to attain academic excellence at that time in my life. Give me a creative assignment, and it's a different story. In fact, my performance in entrepreneurial and non-theory based projects were excellent.

The second reason is that I wasn't convinced I wanted to work at a Big 4 or any other MNC.

It wasn't until my second month at Hult, when entrepreneur / author Jaymin Patel delivered a presentation to the student body called Networking like a rockstar that I could truly appreciate the value of networking. For the first time, networking became "cool", and I was quite good at it too. Furthermore, he outlined some principles that I had unknowingly been practicing. Being likable and having solid people skills helped, and I realised I had a natural inclination to networking since day one.

To my 18 year old self - be a networking rockstar.

2. Be Assertive

In my early years, I've been guilty of jumping into the first opportunity that came my way. Only to find that the opportunity was not for me. A lot of the time, this was due to politeness. Whether it was a social agreement or a network marketing scheme sprung onto me, I never said no.

When I was 18, I worked part time at a surf shop in Brisbane. This provided me with sufficient pocket money during my first year at university. While at this job, I was made to work at the door day after day. Working the door involved checking bags of customers on their way out to ensure they weren't shoplifting. Unsurprisingly, I faced some serious backlash from customers who didn't want their bags checked. In addition, I found it seriously boring standing in the same spot under the air-conditioning and speakers day after day for 6 hours straight. What did I do about it? Nothing. I thought by speaking up and saying no to a door shift, I'd be inconveniencing my supervisors.

Today, I'm a lot more assertive. I say no a lot. And it feels great. I'm freer, more productive, and have more time on my hands to do things that actually serve my purpose.

To my 18 year old self - being assertive is respected, my friend. It shows you have values.

3. Seek Out Mentors

To my 18 year old self, who you know professionally matters more than who you know socially.

I always wanted to work in digital marketing when I was 18. With the rise of search engines and social media, this career was getting more and more competitive. Knowing what I now know, I feel I would've gotten my foot in the door a lot easier than I did. It wouldn't have taken me long to go online and map out the leading CEO's of the digital/ digital marketing space in my city. I'd have then reached out to each one of them to see if I can be a "right-hand man", ie. I'll work for you for free, be on time, and do every editing, revision and research task you need me to do, as long as you promise to teach me everything I need to know to thrive in your industry.

— — —

With this wisdom, knowledge and network, I'd be far more equipped for the real world.

With this in mind, please remember that these are principles we can apply even today, whether it's in our day job or side hustle. As young pros we are fortunate to have time on our side. Therefore, it is not the time for quarter life crisis or regrets. There's no better time to follow our passions, as long as we do not neglect our purpose.

So be resilient in creating your dream career, but be sure to balance it out with practicality by doubling-down on your strengths.

Get In Touch

Reet Sen is an author and marketer at leading UK EdTech company, Full Fabric. Reet visits universities around the world to help optimise student recruitment and admission strategies. If your institution aims to:

- Convert high quality students into applicants
- Enhance administration during the admissions process
- Deliver the best possible student admissions experience

Contact Reet for a free telephone consultation.

reet.sen@fullfabric.com

Enjoyed The Book?

If you found this book valuable, please share it with a friend. It would also mean the world to me if you could leave a comment and a star-rating on the Amazon page.

Connect With The Author

Reach out and say hello!

Instagram: *Reetys*

Snapchat: *Reetys*

Twitter: *ReetSen4*

LinkedIn: *Reet Sen*

Website: *www.reetsen.com*